BONNIE

Romantic Scotland in pictures and verse

Jarrold Colour Publications, Norwich

*Breathes there the man, with soul so dead,
Who never to himself hath said,
   This is my own, my native land!
Whose heart hath ne'er within him burn'd,
As home his footsteps he hath turn'd,
   From wandering on a foreign strand!
If such there breathe, go, mark him well;
For him no Minstrel raptures swell;
High though his titles, proud his name,
Boundless his wealth as wish can claim;
Despite those titles, power, and pelf,
The wretch, concentred all in self,
Living, shall forfeit fair renown,
And, doubly dying, shall go down
To the vile dust, from whence he sprung,
Unwept, unhonour'd, and unsung.*

*O Caledonia! stern and wild,
Meet nurse for a poetic child!
Land of brown heath and shaggy wood,
Land of the mountain and the flood,
Land of my sires! what mortal hand
Can e'er untie the filial band,
That knits me to thy rugged strand!
Still as I view each well-known scene,
Think what is now, and what hath been,
Seems as, to me, of all bereft,
Sole friends thy woods and streams were* **left**;
*And thus I love them better still,
Even in extremity of ill.*

SIR WALTER SCOTT 1771–1832

Opposite: The Pass of Killiecrankie, Tayside

Above and opposite: Wordsworth and Scott immortalised the beauties of St Mary's Loch, Borders, yet it is the local shepherd-poet, James Hogg, who is best remembered here for the sensitivity of his pastoral verses. St Mary's Loch is three miles long and half a mile wide. It is surrounded by steep hills and takes its name from the ancient St Mary's Kirk which stands on its north-west shore

*It was a scene that even the hind
Could not survey with careless mind,
Although accustom'd well to see
Nature in mountain majesty;
For every ray the welkin threw
Slept on St Mary's mirror blue,
In blushing glories out of number,
Like beauty in a mimic slumber.*

Lines by 'The Ettrick Shepherd'
JAMES HOGG 1770–1835

The heath waves wild upon her hills,
  And, foaming frae the fells,
Her fountains sing o' freedom still,
  As they dance down the dells;
And weel I loo the land, my lads,
  That's girded by the sea;—
Then Scotland's vales and Scotland's dales
  And Scotland's hills for me;—
We'll drink a cup to Scotland yet,
  Wi' a' the honours three.

Scotland Yet
HENRY SCOTT RIDDEL 1798–1870

Above: Sunset over Skye with the waiting ferry at Mallaig silhouetted against the rippled surface of the Sound of Sleat. *Opposite:* Quinag from Ullapool, Highland

So thou, fair City! disarray'd
Of battled wall, and rampart's aid,
As stately seem'st, but lovelier far
Than in that panoply of war.
Nor deem that from thy fenceless throne
Strength and security are flown;
Still, as of yore, Queen of the North!
Still canst thou send thy children forth.

Marmion—Canto 5
SIR WALTER SCOTT 1771–1832

Above: The splendid Palace of Holyroodhouse was built in Edinburgh during James IV's reign but was burned in 1543 during an English invasion which left only the north-west tower intact. It was not until Charles II's reign that the Palace was fully reconstructed so the two towers differ in age by 150 years. *Opposite:* The Water of Leith, part of the Old City of Edinburgh

By yon bonnie banks and yon bonnie braes,
  Where the sun shines bright on Loch Lomon';
Oh, we twa hae pass'd sae mony blithesome days,
  On the bonnie, bonnie banks o' Loch Lomon'.

(Chorus): Oh! ye'll tak' the high road and I'll tak' the
  low road,
    An' I'll be in Scotland before ye;
  But wae is my heart until we meet again,
    On the bonnie, bonnie banks o' Loch Lomon'.

          The bonnie banks o' Loch Lomon'.
                    TRADITIONAL JACOBITE AIR

Above: Loch Lomond and the Trossachs. Lòch Lomond is the largest inland lake in Britain. *Opposite:* The Grey Mare's Tail is a dramatic 200-foot waterfall in Dumfries and Galloway

Above: Scotland still enthusiastically supports her own culture; the bagpipes are frequently to be heard in town and country, a sound very much enjoyed by the initiated. *Opposite:* The 'bristly' country of the Trossachs owes much of its fame to Scott's marvellous accounts of its scenery in *Rob Roy* and *The Lady of the Lake*. Loch Achray, seen here, is one of the loveliest lochs of the district

In the highlands, in the country places,
Where the old plain men have rosy faces,
And the young fair maidens
Quiet eyes;
Where essential silence cheers and blesses,
And for ever in the hill-recesses
Her more lovely music
Broods and dies.

                Songs of Travel
                ROBERT LOUIS STEVENSON 1850–1894

The smiling spring comes in rejoicing,
  And surly winter grimly flies:
Now crystal clear are the falling waters,
  And bonnie blue are the sunny skies;
Fresh o'er the mountains breaks forth the morning,
  The ev'ning gilds the ocean's swell;
All creatures joy in the sun's returning,
  And I rejoice in my bonnie Bell.

Bonnie Bell
ROBERT BURNS 1759–1796

Above: Kilchurn Castle, Strathclyde, is situated on Loch Awe beneath massive Ben Cruachan (3,689 feet). It dates from the mid-fifteenth century and is one of the most romantic ruins in Scotland

Above: The Trossachs, Central, are famous as the inspiration for Scott's poem *The Lady of the Lake*. They are a romantic wooded defile between Loch Achray and Loch Katrine

A birr! a whirr! the salmon's out,
  Far on the rushing river;
Onward he holds with sudden leap,
Or plunges through the whirlpool deep,
  A desperate endeavour!
    Hark to the music of the reel!
      The fitful and the grating;
    It pants along the breathless wheel,
      Now hurried—now abating.

The Taking of the Salmon
THOMAS TOD STODDART 1810–1880

The River Dochart, Killin, Central

Mildly and soft the western breeze
Just kiss'd the Lake, just stirr'd the trees,
And the pleased lake, like maiden coy,
Trembled but dimpled not for joy;
The mountain shadows on her breast
Were neither broken nor at rest;
In bright uncertainty they lie,
Like future joys to Fancy's eye.

> The Lady of the Lake
> SIR WALTER SCOTT 1771–1832

Above: The pleasure-steamer *Sir Walter Scott* moored at the pier on Loch Katrine, Central. *Opposite:* Abbotsford House was the home of Sir Walter Scott from 1812 until his death in 1832. His rooms have remained unchanged and contain a library of more than 20,000 rare books and his collection of historical relics

Above: Callander, gateway to the Highlands, with Ben Ledi (2,785 feet) guarding the main route northwards. *Opposite:* Ben More and Strathfillan, Central

My native Scotland! Oh, thy northern hills,
  Thy dark brown hills, are fondly dear to me;
And aye a warmth my swelling bosom fills
  For all the filial souls that cling to thee!
  Pure be their loves as human love can be;
And still be worthy of their native land
  The little beings nursed beside their knee,—
What may at length their country's guardians stand,
And own the undaunted heart, and lift the unconquer'd hand!

> The Wooer's Visit
> WILLIAM KNOX 1789–1825

When daisies go, shall winter time
Silver the simple grass with rime;
Autumnal frosts enchant the pool
And make the cart-ruts beautiful;
And when snow-bright the moor expands,
How shall your children clap their hands!
To make this earth, our hermitage,
A cheerful and a changeful page,
God's bright and intricate device
Of days and seasons doth suffice.

The House Beautiful
ROBERT LOUIS STEVENSON 1850–1894

Above: The Braemar Gathering, Grampian, dates from 1832 when it was initiated by the Braemar Wrights' Friendly Society. *Opposite:* Crathie Church, Grampian, is often attended by the Royal Family when they stay at nearby Balmoral Castle

It's hame, and it's hame, hame fain wad I be,
An' it's hame, hame, hame, to my ain countree!
When the flower is i' the bud and the leaf is on the tree,
The lark shall sing me hame in my ain countree;
It's hame, and it's hame, hame fain wad I be,
An' it's hame, hame, hame, to my ain countree!

It's Hame, and it's Hame
ALLAN CUNNINGHAM 1784–1842

Above: Sunset over Loch Torridon which lies on the mainland opposite Skye. *Opposite:* Loch Eck, Strathclyde, is situated in the Cowal Peninsula, an area indented with great sea-lochs stretching from Loch Fyne to the Firth of Clyde

From scenes like these old Scotia's grandeur springs,
  That makes her loved at home, revered abroad;
Princes and lords are but the breath of kings,
  'An honest man's the noblest work of God':
And certes, in fair virtue's heavenly road,
  The cottage leaves the palace far behind;
What is a lordling's pomp?—a cumbrous load,
  Disguising oft the wretch of human kind,
Studied in arts of hell, in wickedness refined!

The Cotter's Saturday Night
ROBERT BURNS 1759–1796

Above: A 'Black House' at Luib, Isle of Skye. This was once a common form of thatched housing on the island with wall cavities several feet wide filled with earth. *Opposite:* The Falls of Rogie are situated on the Blackwater River, two miles north-west of Contin, Highland

Above: The spectacular Applecross road over Bealach nam Ba, Ross and Cromarty, is one of the highest mountain roads in Scotland with a summit of 2,053 feet and steep zigzag turns

My heart's in the Highlands, my heart is not here;
My heart's in the Highlands a-chasing the deer;
Chasing the wild deer, and following the roe,
My heart's in the Highlands, wherever I go.
Farewell to the Highlands, farewell to the North,
The birth-place of valour, the country of worth;
Wherever I wander, wherever I rove,
The hills of the Highlands for ever I love.

                        My Heart's in the Highlands
                        ROBERT BURNS 1759–1796

Above: The Red Deer is a denizen of the high moors and mountains. The females and their young roam in separate herds to the stags and during the rutting season the mountains echo with their eerie calls

Now westlin winds and slaughtering guns
  Bring autumn's pleasant weather;
The moorcock springs, on whirring wings,
  Amang the blooming heather:
Now waving grain, wide o'er the plain,
  Delights the weary farmer;
And the moon shines bright, when I rove at night
  To muse upon my charmer.

Now Westlin Winds
ROBERT BURNS 1759–1796

Above: The beauty of the wild heather at Loch Na Craige, Tayside, is matched by the rugged scenery of Cul Beag and Stack Polly above Stoer Bay, Highland, *(opposite)*, an area popular for trout-fishing

Go, little book, and wish to all
Flowers in the garden, meat in the hall,
A bin of wine, a spice of wit,
A house with lawns enclosing it,
A living river by the door,
A nightingale in the sycamore!
    Envoy
    ROBERT LOUIS STEVENSON 1850–1894

Above: Allan Ramsay, 1685–1758, is remembered in Edinburgh – where he operated a successful bookseller's business – by this statue in Princes Street gardens. His claim to fame is through his poetry, by which he gained great popularity